MW00880648

Executive Skills Workbook for Teens

Ultimate workbook for Teens/Adults to self-regulate, reduce negative thoughts, boost inner strength, and improve self-management for future life.

BY

Harvey Paul
ASH Publisher

About the Author

Harvey Paul is a well-known name in the world of ebooks regarding teen mindset-related concerns. The author has extensive knowledge in this field and is skilled at making a quick impression on readers. He is an expert in teaching teens growth mindsets. The most effective advice and methods for removing entrenched attitudes. His writings guarantee that the readers will receive high-quality and latest information. To empower teenagers to take care of themselves, Aubin makes sure to write useful and solution-focused books.

Contents

Introduction

Executive abilities include mind abilities that involve forming plans, solving problems, and making decisions. Additionally, it supports adolescent focus, rule memory, temptation resistance, and flexible thinking. Our brains' executive functioning mechanisms enable us to carry out daily duties. They include our capacity for task prioritization, material organization, activity focus, and grit under pressure. These abilities are crucial and should be considered. We utilize these abilities frequently each day without even realizing it. Every person has a different set of executive functioning strengths and challenges. Executive functioning issues might therefore affect different people in different ways. While certain actions may be overt, others may be restrained.

Mind skills that involve formulating plans, resolving issues, and making judgments are considered executive talents. Additionally, it helps adolescents maintain attention, remember rules, resist temptation, and think creatively. We can perform daily tasks because of the executive functioning processes in our brains. They include our ability to prioritize tasks, organize materials, maintain activity focus, and remain composed under duress. It should be obvious that these skills are important. Without ever realizing it, we use these skills all day long. The strengths and challenges of executive functioning vary from person to person. Therefore, different people may be impacted by executive functioning difficulties differently. While some activities might be obvious, others might be more covert.

These abilities do not come pre-developed in children, but they do have the potential to do so. For developing these skills, some kids might require more assistance than others. In other cases, children's skill development can be significantly slowed down or impeded if they do not receive the support they require from their connections with people and the circumstances in their settings or (worse) if such influences are sources of toxic stress. Children who grow up in unfortunate conditions brought on by neglect, abuse, or violence may experience the negative effects of stress, which can alter their brain's architecture and inhibit the growth of executive ability.

One of society's most significant duties is to give children the assistance they need to develop these skills at home, in early care and education programs. Children are given support in surroundings that support their growth, allowing them to practice the required abilities before doing so on their own. By forming and upholding supportive, dependable relationships, setting routines, and serving as social role models, adults can help children develop their executive function abilities. Children should also practice their skills through activities that encourage imaginative play and social interaction, teach them how to manage stress, require vigorous exercise, and eventually give them opportunities to take more responsibility for their actions with less adult supervision.

A Note to Teens

Hi Teens!

You may notice that all of us come into contact with a variety of talents daily, including:

√ Active memory

√ Flexible thought

√ Self-control

√ Focus

√ Observing guidelines

√ Controlling feelings

Looking at this list made me understand how crucial executive functioning skills are for all kids' teens, and tweens, and even we need all these skills our whole life.

Executive functioning abilities are not innate in humans. We acquire executive functions throughout our lives through a variety of events. Frequently through the experiences we offer in the classroom! However, teacher preparation programs do not give executive functioning adequate attention. Executive functioning abilities are not innate in humans.

At different phases of life, we learn how to use our executive functions through various experiences, frequently through ones we give to others in school. However, teacher preparation programs do not give executive functioning adequate attention. Our brains are intricate devices that continually create connections or communication routes that allow one region of the brain to signal or communicate with another. For example, in the part of the mind, executive functioning skills are developed. That part of the brain is responsible for creating.

The linkages emerging from our experiences and learning are formed in that brain area. The relationships start in early childhood and get stronger as we age and enter adulthood. During the process, we establish our fundamental competencies, which are called executive functional competencies.

Like working out any other muscle in the body, strengthening our brain connections strengthens our executive functioning abilities. Through routine and modeling, we can assist our kids in learning these skills and using them in their daily lives.

Dear teens, It will be better for you if you keep some things in mind that executive function abilities develop differently in different minds. Developing these skills may require more direct assistance for some pupils than for their peers. Learning and executive function can be hampered by stress.

Chapter 1. Executive Skills

Young people need executive skills to function freely. They consist of goal-setting, goal-setting, task-initiation, task organization, sustained attention, problem-solving, and planning. The decision-making part of the brain is still developing and will keep doing so until roughly age 25.

As a result, adolescents' ability to make mature decisions is typically trumped by intuitive instincts rather than critical reasoning. Self-control, working memory, emotion regulation, attention, task initiation, planning or prioritization, organization, time management, establishing and accomplishing goals, flexibility, observation, and Stress tolerance are the twelve executive functioning skills.

1.1 Term Executive Function Mean

Executive functioning abilities are also referred to as the brain's management system. They are a group of mental abilities that include working memory, self-control, and flexible thinking. Students who struggle with executive functioning may find concentrating and following instructions challenging, impacting their learning ability. However, executive functioning teaching benefits students at all performance levels for various reasons.

Poor executive functioning is characterized by difficulties organizing, planning, prioritizing, staying focused and involved in tasks, as well as difficulties controlling emotions, self-monitoring, and understanding the perspectives of others. An executive functioning disorder may have trouble focusing, staying organized, finishing work, and interacting with others appropriately and under control. By imparting these skills at a young age, we can address issues that inevitably arise before joining the workforce.

1.2 What Are Executive Skills for Teens

Executive function skills are frequently difficult for children with learning difficulties, which can make it difficult for them to recall important information and to plan, organize, and finish projects effectively. In addition, kids with poor executive function abilities may have an inadequate working memory, which is the capacity to analyze and prioritize information in real-time temporarily. Learn how to help your child's executive function and working memory through practice and repetition in the suggestions and tactics below.

As we gain more understanding of how the brain develops throughout a person's lifetime, it seems to sense that exercising our working memory can enhance performance, just as we do with other muscles. If your child has problems recalling multi-step directions that are appropriate for their age or switching between jobs, think about If your child has problems following age-appropriate multi-step directions or switching between projects you might want to assist them in practicing switching tasks by switching tasks and having them switch back and forth. For instance, if your child has a reading or writing project to finish, have them alternate between both the task and a puzzle until both are finished. The capacity of your child to switch between tasks should become simpler with experience, even if this exercise may first strain their limitations. Technology use can also aid in strengthening working memory.

1.3 Importance of Executive Functioning Skills

Throughout life, executive function skills are crucial. People and society gain again for the rest of their lives when youngsters are given a chance to have executive function and self-regulation skills.

Executive function abilities aid students in following complicated instructions, avoiding distractions, readjusting when rules change, persevering with problem-solving, and managing lengthy tasks.

The result is a population that is more educated and prepared to handle the problems of the twenty-first century for society.

Executive functions assist young people in acquiring abilities such as collaboration, leadership, goal-setting, decision-making, critical thinking, flexibility, and self-awareness of one's own and others' emotions. As a result, greater social cohesion, less crime, and more stable regions are the results for society.

People with executive function abilities can better resist pressure to take risks, use drugs, or engage in unprotected sex and be more aware of the safety of their children. Having strong executive function prepares our bodies and coping mechanisms to handle stress. A healthier population, a more effective workforce, and lower healthcare costs are the results for society.

Executive function abilities boost our chances of achieving economic success because they help us to be more organized, address difficulties that call for planning, and be ready to change course when necessary. In addition, more prosperity for society results from a creative, skilled, and adaptable workforce.

1.4 Ways to Develop Executive Functioning Skills

The phrase "executive function" refers to a group of mental operations that enable us to link prior experience with current behavior. When we plan, organize, strategize, pay attention to and remember specifics, and more, we are using executive function. Our ability to focus our attention, block out distractions, and shift mental gears depends on our executive function abilities. Effective time management is a component of executive function as well.

These abilities enable us to do our work on time, request assistance when necessary, hold our tongue until called upon and look for additional information.

Exercises for The Executive Function

√ Concentrate on endeavors that improve the planning procedure. For example, it can be accomplished by learning how to do the laundry, which involves several steps.

√ Exercise with strategy games and mental challenges. Logic puzzles and strategy games improve the learning process, organization, and concentration. For this, Settlers of Catan is a fantastic game.

√ Yoga and meditation help people pay attention for longer periods, lower stress and make better decisions.

√ Instruction in study skills enhances planning, time management, and self-awareness.

√ Sports like tennis, football, and laser tag that require constant environment awareness enhance executive function abilities.

√ Singing, dancing, and playing an instrument enhance inhibition, cognitive flexibility, and attention.

√ The Sentence Zone, solving puzzles, arithmetic and number puzzles, and spatially puzzles like Rubik's Cubes all help to increase working memory and mental and cognitive flexibility.

1.5 Importance of Executive Functioning Skills for Students

Flexible Thought

A child with adaptable thinking skills can solve problems, adapt to circumstances, and get through immediate challenges. This ability also pertains to a child's capacity to consider other people's viewpoints.

Planning

A child's capacity for planning, prioritizing various tasks, and thinking about the future are all excellent indicators of cognitive growth. For example, a child with planning skills may develop a list of actions to complete a task and can accurately decide the most crucial components.

Self-Control

The ability of a youngster to manage their physical or emotional outbursts is referred to as self-control. Impulse control prevents children from responding or acting without thinking. In contrast, emotional control enables them to maintain their composure and avoid the impulse to shut down or overreact in the face of setbacks or challenges.

Working Memory Working memory refers to a child's capacity to remember and store information to use later. Given that it is in charge of short-term memory and execution, this ability is essential for a youngster to succeed in the classroom.

Management of Time

The ability of a youngster to create an effective schedule, complete tasks on time, and use tolerance when focusing on schoolwork is referred to as time management. Because it is necessary for many circumstances, children must learn how to manage their time.

Organization

A youngster's capacity to efficiently arrange objects or ideas in an ordered manner is called organization abilities. Being organized helps children learn how to tell stories clearly and keep track of their belongings, which is essential for their development and growth.

Chapter 2. Self-Regulation in Teens

Self-regulation is now understood to play a crucial role in fostering welfare throughout life, including physical, emotional, social, and economic health and academic success.

Self-regulation is the process of controlling one's thoughts and emotions to permit main objective behavior, such as the range of behaviors necessary for success in the job, relationships, and academic settings. As better self-regulation predicts higher income, better financial planning, less risky behaviors like substance use and aggression, and lower health expenditures, supporting the development of self-regulation in youth is an investment in society.

There are periods during this development when the effects of hormones magnify the sensation of emotion. Self-regulation is developed and taught through interactions with caregivers and the larger community.

Self-regulation is a skill developed and acquired over a long period, from infancy through young adulthood, through interactions with caregivers and the surrounding environment. Like education, cognitive, emotional, and behavioral self-regulation abilities can be taught with structure, encouragement, and coaching over time. Effective interventions can help youth with difficulties or delays with self-regulation, and there are always possibilities to intervene at different stages of development.

2.1 Self-Regulation and Its Important

For pupils with high ability levels, self-regulated learning is essential. It is so that it supports their pursuit of excellence. Excellence can only be attained with practice. Planning, effort, and patience are required for this over time. Self-controlled learning aids in this procedure. It enables them to develop into independent learners who can follow their interests.

High-ability pupils can participate in challenging activities. These tasks might need more advanced degrees of self-regulated learning. A student's aptitude in a topic matter and their capacity for self-control may not match. These students may require more complex self-regulated learning techniques. They will be better able to complete challenging jobs.

Self-Regulation is important to:

√ Establishing more ambitious objectives

√ Using increasingly sophisticated tools for self-monitoring

√ Modeling more sophisticated learning techniques,

√ Or by asking more challenging contemplation questions.

High-ability pupils must be given activities that are quite challenging if they are to have the chance to practice self-regulation.

2.2 How and When to Improve Self-Regulation in Teens

Students choose, monitor, and employ learning practices using self-regulation mechanisms. Early on, successful students often develop the ability to self-regulate their learning; they know when, how, and why to apply a certain technique. Unfortunately, many students who struggle with learning tend to forget academic skills or use the same, frequently inefficient strategy for all academic work.

These pupils must take ownership of their education if they are to succeed. They can achieve this by developing the ability to control their conduct. In the table below, four self-regulation techniques are emphasized.

√ Self-monitoring

√ Self-instruction

√ Goal-setting

√ Self-reinforcement

These tactics can be utilized individually, but they can also be used in tandem. For instance, a learner can combine self-instruction with self-monitoring. If the learner is not improving, he should consider why and discuss it with himself. He might also tell himself that he will work harder and perform better the next time by self-instruction. You can integrate self-regulation techniques successfully with other techniques.

2.3 Helping Teenagers Learn and Practice Self-Regulation

Your childhood affects how well you can control yourself as an adult. 2 kids must develop self-control since it promotes maturity and social ties. For example, a toddler with tantrums learns to accept difficult feelings without acting out. Likewise, a teen can manage impulses and respond calmly to uncomfortable feelings when developing into an adult.

In essence, maturity is the capacity to respond patiently and thoughtfully to emotional, social, and cognitive dangers in the environment. It's not a coincidence that this description made you think of mindfulness because self-regulation is a key component of mindfulness.

The benefits of assisting children and teenagers in developing self-regulation abilities are enormous. These abilities can support children and young adults in various ways, including helping them complete their tasks and chores, keep their friendships strong, and make safe decisions. At the same time, they go out with friends, prevent themself from breaking the law, persevere through obstacles once they feel like giving up, and much more.

2.4 How Parents Can Help Teens to Enhance Their Self-Regulation

Self-regulation entails a collection of abilities that enable us to control our strong emotions and deliberate before acting. Here are some tips on encouraging children's development of regulating abilities.

You should work on your stress management. Have your own needs taken care of so you can help kids and provide a fine example for them.

Keep your eye on the results. The ultimate objective is not merely to reduce children's problematic behavior. Our goal is to impart skills. Children's behavior will improve when they learn stress management techniques. You'll observe that they are abler to manage environmental changes and tolerate stress.

Create reasonable expectations. Analyze the skills of the kids to see where they need help. Remember that younger children's brains are less developed and have less self-control. Demand as much as they can bear from kids while remembering that success breeds success. Be prepared for development and learning obstacles.

Keep your cool and demonstrate self-control. Remember that when kids react in the heat of the moment, they are operating in survival mode. Their lower minds are working nonstop. They are incapable of understanding reason or logic, therefore, do not attempt to reason with them. Instead, remain composed, demonstrate empathy, assist them in developing self-awareness, and lead them through more sensory stimuli and calming techniques.

Be encouraging and supportive. As youngsters learn to regulate, they feel loved, appreciated, and understood. Display your concern and interaction with them as a concerned mentor or counselor.

Make sure to replenish the children's resource pool for regulation frequently. The three pillars of good health are rest, nutrition, and exercise. Assist kids in making plans for activities they excel at and like.

Reduce irrational demands. Check the kids' schedules to ensure they are not too busy. Too many obligations will make kids more stressed and make it harder for them to control their energy levels.

Ensure order and uniformity. Teach kids what is expected of them and what to anticipate from you, e.g., practices, strong directions, and practice schedules. Having predictability reduces stress.

Work together to make learning about regulation enjoyable. Use creativity when assisting kids with developing, applying, and adapting coping mechanisms for regulation. Consider their suggestions. Describe the working protocol in terms they can comprehend. For instance, if kids enjoy science, Give them this assignment as a test. Make it seem like a mission if they enjoy espionage video games.

Inform kids about their brains. Help them to comprehend how both the upstairs and downstairs brains influence the control of their stress response.

Increase the vocabulary. Children should be asked about their feelings. Inform them of their available resources.

Increase their awareness of themselves to aid in self-monitoring. Help kids rate their energy level and emotions on a scale from 1 (low) to 5 (high). Assist them in identifying calming techniques and ways to replenish their supply of resources.

Assist them in building a toolkit of coping mechanisms for when they become dysregulated. The goal is to teach kids to pause, be cool, and consider rather than act on strong emotions.

2.5 Behavioral Self-Regulation Versus Cognitive Self-Regulation

Self-regulation refers to the capacity to manage one's actions, feelings, and ideas while pursuing long-term objectives. Emotional self-regulation is the capacity to restrain irrational emotions and impulses or deliberate before acting.

Self-regulation also entails being able to bounce back from setbacks and behave morally. Is it one of the five essential modules of social awareness? Developing a range of beneficial habits that influence how one uses cognitive talents to incorporate learning processes is a key component of cognitive self-regulation.

These procedures are designed and modified to achieve individual objectives in dynamic situations. It entails exercising control over various mental tactics to enhance cognitive performance. It can be considered metacognition because it involves controlling one's thought process. Cognitive self-regulation is a way of learning that involves adaptive competence, persistence, and self-initiative. Psychomotor retardation in patients may be lessened if significant effort is put into developing greater self-regulation abilities in people with schizophrenia.

Chapter 3. Reduce Negative Thoughts and Boost Inner Strength

People can learn simple ways to assist them in getting rid of that critical voice and increase their life's joy, vitality, and connections.

Wait Additional

Pause if you're experiencing tension or anxiety or are thinking negatively. Use all five senses to focus your attention on the environment around you.

Recognize the Change

Observe the difference between being engrossed in your thoughts and being present in the moment by using all of your senses. Also, take note of your mental activities.

Write Down Your Ideas

If it isn't, try taking a step back and labeling your thoughts rather than taking them as literal truths.

Keep doing this labeling exercise without seeking to soften, alter, or steer clear of any particular thoughts. Instead, note what it feels like to be somewhat separated from your thoughts as the thinker.

Pick an Objective

You are better able to choose your intention and the next appropriate step for you once you have paused from your mental struggle, noticed what's happening and how it has been operating and labeled your ideas for what they are simple, temporary mental weather.

3.1 Stop Negative Self-Talk to Reduce Stress

The constant chatter and thoughts in your head are known as self-talk. It may assume a variety of personas, including those of your inner kid, inner cheerleader, inner grownup, or inner critic. Every one of us engages in self-talk regularly. It frequently connects to prior events, underlying assumptions, and skewed thought processes. Self-talk can be fueled by negative ideas and sentiments and can significantly affect one's sense of self and how one sees the world. Negative self-talk has a significant negative effect on self-esteem and unhealthy habits, which can exacerbate problems like mental illness and addiction problems.

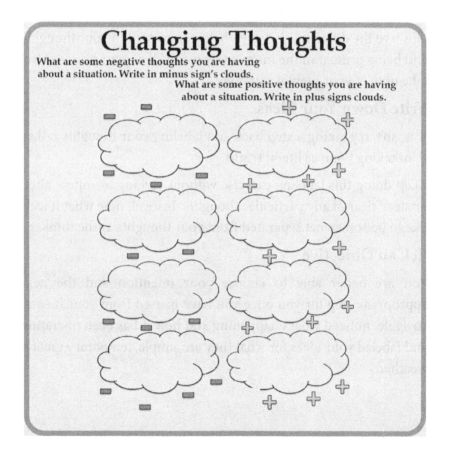

Changing Thoughts

What are some negative thoughts you are having about a situation. Write in minus sign's clouds.

What are some positive thoughts you are having about a situation. Write in plus signs clouds.

3.2 Understanding Positive Thinking and Self-Talk

In simple words, positive thinking means difficult approaching circumstances in a positive and proactive manner. Instead of expecting the worst, you hope for the best.

Positive thinking typically starts with self-talk. Self-talk is the constant internal communication that takes place. It's possible to think about anything positive or unpleasant automatically. You use logic and reason in some things you say to yourself. Other self-talk may result from inferences you draw based on a lack of information or anticipations sparked by preconceived conceptions of what might happen. Your attitude on life is more likely to be negative if most of your opinions are destructive. If your ideas are generally positive, you probably consider yourself an optimist or someone who engages in positive thinking.

3.3 The Health Benefits of Positivity

There is still a study on the effects of optimism and positive thinking on health. A number of health benefits of positive thinking include extended life, lowered incidence of depression, Improved physical and mental health; increased resistance to infections; decreased levels of anxiety and discomfort; decreased risk of death from heart disease and stroke; improved cardiovascular health; decreased risk of dying from cancer; decreased risk of dying from respiratory diseases; decreased risk of infection-related mortality; and improved coping mechanisms for challenges and stressful situations.

It's unclear why positive thinkers experience these health benefits.

One theory holds that keeping a positive viewpoint makes it simpler to deal with challenging situations and lessens the damaging effects of stress on your body's health.

Furthermore, it is thought that upbeat people lead better lives. This is because they engage in increased physical activity, eat a well-balanced diet, refrain from smoking, and limit alcohol intake.

3.4 Practice Mindfulness and Self-Awareness

Self-care methods like mindfulness can help us control our thoughts more effectively. With the help of these methods, we can take care of ourselves even when we are really busy. By calling our attention to the feeling of every inhalation at the point of the nostrils or the rise and fall of our abdomen as we breathe in and out, mindfulness practices frequently concentrate mostly on the rhythm of our breathing.

The first stage in effective leadership is cultivating emotional self-awareness, which is the basis for the remaining Emotional and Social Intelligence Competencies. If we don't have emotional self-awareness, we can't learn abilities like emotional self-control, empathy, or teamwork. In addition, it provides leaders with the knowledge they need about themselves and the success of their relationships so they can keep an eye on their emotions and adjust their conduct as necessary.

Practice Mindfulness and Self-Awareness

1	Mindful coloring
2	Connect with nature
3	Dragon breathing
4	Smell the flowers breathing
5	Practice yoga
6	Mindfulness 5-4-3-2-1
7	Positive affirmations
8	Guided meditations
9	Use breathing visuals
10	Listen to music

3.5 Getting to Know Your Inner Strength

Your capacity to carry out tasks correctly is a sign of inner strength. It entails doing duties and making decisions without regard for the opinions of those around you to accomplish your top priorities. Internal fortitude is:

√ inner tenacity

√ possessing willpower

√ self-control

√ the capacity to overcome challenges

√ and impediments

Most people give out the battery physically or emotionally, which gives you enough strength to keep trying. However, to achieve your life dreams, you must possess inner strength.

Anyone who utilizes their inner power exhibits serenity, consideration, tranquillity, and patience. To use such discipline throughout your life, you need to have the endurance that the word durable normally connotes.

It is crucial to comprehend since living the life of your dreams depends on your inner power. You can overcome the challenges life will provide you with by drawing on your inner power. When you think of a strong sense of inner power and purpose, words like endurance and resilience come to mind.

My Strengths

Things I am good at:

1 _____

2 _____

3 _____

Compliments I have received:

1 _____

2 _____

3 _____

What I like about my appearance:

1 _____

2 _____

3 _____

Challenges I have overcome:

1 _____

2 _____

3 _____

I've helped others by:

1 _____

2 _____

3 _____

Things that make me unique:

1 _____

2 _____

3 _____

What I value the most:

1 _____

2 _____

3 _____

Times I've made others happy:

1 _____

2 _____

3 _____

3.6 Handling Negative Thoughts

Negative thinking can factor in issues including low self-esteem, melancholy, stress, and social anxiety. Understanding how you think currently and the matters that happen is the key to changing your negative thoughts. After that, utilize techniques to alter these thoughts or lessen their impact.

Meditation is the practice of mindfulness. It involves the practice of distancing yourself from your ideas and emotions so that you may examine them objectively. You can increase your self-awareness and become more aware of your thoughts by engaging in mindfulness practices.

Mindfulness's goal is to alter how you interact with your thoughts. Consider your thoughts and emotions as things that are passing by that you can stop and observe or let go of.

Handling Negative Thoughts

What makes me feel sad

Thought I have

How my body reacts

What helpp me stay calm

Who can I go to for help

Questions to ask myself

Is the situation out of my control?
YES ☐ NO ☐
Is the safety of myself or others at risk?
YES ☐ NO ☐
Can something positive come of the situation?
YES ☐ NO ☐
Can I do anything to change what is happening?
YES ☐ NO ☐

3.7 Positive Self-Talk Journal

In positive self-talk, you talk to your inner self positively. It exposes emotions, opinions, concerns, and ideas and is impacted by your subconscious mind. Optimism and positive thinking can be powerful pressure strategies. It is true that having a more optimistic attitude in life has some favorable effects on your health.

Your productivity and overall health can both benefit from self-talk. For instance, studies demonstrate that self-talk can improve athletic performance. They might benefit from having more endurance or being able to lift more weight. A more upbeat mindset and constructive self-talk can also have the following additional health advantages:

√   Heightened liveliness

√   Higher satisfaction with life

√   Enhanced immunological response

√   Higher physical well-being,

√   Better cardiovascular health,

√   Lower mortality risk

√   Less stress and anxiety

Positive Self-Talk Journal

I felt good when...	I am proud of myself because...	Something that went well today was...
I had fun when...	This makes me unique...	I learned from this mistake...
I feel strong when...	The best part of today was...	A good quality I am learning is...
This was interesting today...	Something I am grateful for is...	A way I was kind today was...
An accomplishment I made this week was...	I like this about myself...	Something I love about my life is...

3.8 Boosting Cognitive Flexibility

The ability to transition between jobs or responsibilities in response to environmental changes is flexibility. It refers to adapting our behavior to various environmental stimuli or settings. Researchers also refer to executive functionality as cognitive flexibility, shifting, task switching, or mental flexibility. A crucial life skill is mental flexibility.

Moreover, it is possible to learn how to be mentally flexible. When our thinking becomes inflexible, we invariably experience constrained perceptions and actions and increase our stress. There are numerous strategies to develop mental agility. For example, you can solve jigsaw puzzles, fix a malfunctioning paper shredder, or prepare food using different ingredients. You can also engage in mindfulness.

If you become better at being flexible, how do you think
it can help your relationships and interactions?
Put your ideas in thought bubbles.

Chapter 4. Improving Self-Management for Future Life

For any business to succeed, talent and knowledge advancement are crucial. Although, certain abilities should take precedence. Self-management abilities are undoubtedly one of them.

Self-management skill development is an ongoing process that is both exciting and difficult. An adolescent would benefit much from learning self-management skills and understanding the methods for acquiring these abilities.

Teenagers likely believe that being self-reliant entails having self-management skills. But that's only a portion of it. In actuality, it signifies your capacity to assume personal accountability. A few examples of self-management abilities are:

√ Time management,

√ Decision-making,

√ Problem-solving,

√ Organizational skills,

√ Stress management,

√ Health Administration

As you can see, developing good self-management techniques will benefit teens in more ways than one. They may enhance every aspect of their lives thanks to it.

4.1 Self-Management for Teens

Self-management may sound like having a boss, but starting your firm is unnecessary. It actually entails doing the best you can while accepting accountability for your actions. You decide to go above and beyond what is necessary.

Self-management demonstrates your ability to plan and contribute unique thoughts to any project. You take notes, arrive promptly, and plan. Becoming the master of Yourself, as opposed to a team or business, is the goal.

Self Management Skills

Breathing & Relaxation	Emotional Healing	Self Motivation	Physical Well Being
*Step one to self management	*Addressing underlying causes	*Be a good friend to yourself	*Relationship with your body
*Diaphragm breathing	*Inner child imagery	*Targeted affirmations	*Relationship with food
*Deep breathing exercise	*Revisiting & revising memories	*Positive self talk	*The hard part gets easier
*Relaxation techniques	*Positive connection with yourself	*Mental rehearsal & positive imagery	*Positive vision and new habits

4.2 Self-Management Skills Enhancement

The main goal of social and emotional learning competencies is to provide students with the tools they need to live successfully. Along with other enduring skills, self-assurance, social and emotional awareness, and self-awareness are taught in character education. However, among the most important abilities that pupils learn can be self-management.

Goal-setting

Students and teachers should work together to define small, doable objectives that each student can pursue. For example, goals might range from functioning gently for a set time to consistently handing in schoolwork.

Behavior Observation

Students engage in self-monitoring, also known as behavior monitoring, when they keep track of their actions and correct them as needed. As a result, they develop their self-awareness abilities and keep track of their setbacks and victories. Students can better understand where they struggle and where they excel by self-monitoring.

Self-Reinforcement

The act of rewarding oneself is known as self-reinforcement. Self-reinforcement is known as rewarding oneself after engaging in the intended behavior or realizing a goal. Rewarding good behavior makes it more likely that your kid will repeat it.

Self-evaluation

Although students may eagerly anticipate the benefits, they learn the most when they reflect on the process. Teachers and students can acquire confidence in their abilities using these questions and replies. They can also point out areas where both the instructor and the pupil feel they can make improvements.

Executive Skills Checklist

Below you will find a list of common school challenge.
Please rate each one on a scale of 1 (not a problem) to 5 (a big problem).
Your answers will help you to scale your executive skills and you can
take help to improve that skills.

Response Inhibition

1 2 3 4 5 _____ Rushing through work just to get it done

1 2 3 4 5 _____ Not having the patience to produce quality work

1 2 3 4 5 _____ Giving up on a homework assignment when I encounter an obstacle

1 2 3 4 5 _____ Avoiding or not completing homework when there are more fun things to do

Working Memory

1 2 3 4 5 _____ Writing down instructions without enough details to understand later

1 2 3 4 5 _____ Forgetting to take home or school necessary materials

1 2 3 4 5 _____ Forgetting to do important task

1 2 3 4 5 _____ Forgetting long time projects or upcoming tests

1 2 3 4 5 _____ Not paying attention to classroom instructions

1 2 3 4 5 _____ Trouble remembering multiple directions

1 2 3 4 5 _____ Losing materials

1 2 3 4 5 _____ Forgetting to complete assignments

1 2 3 4 5 _____ Forgetting to check agenda or assignments

1 2 3 4 5 _____ Forgetting when an assignment is due

4.3 Examples of Self-Management Skills

Examples of self-management skills are as under.

Time Management

When you manage your time, you control how you spend it. It entails managing your daily to-do list and putting your most crucial things first.

Self-Motivation

Your capacity to get inspired and proactively complete daily chores are referred to as self-motivation. Developing your motivation can assist you in becoming more self-aware and prioritizing the things that are essential to you, but it does need some personal accountability.

Stress Management

You must practice healthy stress management to be good at self-management. Without managing stress, you may get burnout due to overwork.

Adaptability

Being adaptive entails having the self-assurance and flexibility to shift course when necessary. It is fundamental for teens working in a dynamic workplace where project changes happen frequently.

Decision Making

If teens are to succeed, they must possess decision-making skills that reduce uncertainty and increase team enablement. Solving problems and meeting obstacles might help you become better at making decisions.

Goal Alignment

You can order the tasks according to their importance and business impact by establishing objectives. Long-term, this will produce greater results and strengthen team spirit.

Personal development

Personal development is crucial for all team members, especially for leaders. You must first develop your expertise before you can develop the knowledge of your colleagues. Improve your management abilities; this entails making the time to attend workshops, enroll in courses, and network with business leaders.

4.4 Ways to Improve Self-Management Skills

You can develop good self-management skills by identifying your strengths, keeping yourself organized, and setting goals.

√ Give your health and well-being priority.

√ Know your areas of strength.

√ Pay attention to one task at once.

√ Create an organizational framework.

√ Define your own short- and long-term objectives.

Ways to Improve Self-Management Skills

Time	Activity	What it looks like(suggestions)
	Wake up	Eat a nutrious breakfast
	Morning Routine	Make your bed. Get dressed. Brush your teeth.
	Academic Time	Do any work assigned by your teacher to you.
	Creative Time	No technology. Use this time to draw, paint build with legos, or play an instrument.
	Lunch Time	Eat a healthy lunch.
	Chore Time	Sort and fold laundary, dust sweep.
	Academic Time	Do any work assigned by your teacher(s). Read for at least 20 minutes. Write in a journal.
	Free Time	Go outside, participate in a sport.
	Community Service Time	Write a letter to someone in a nursing home. Walk a pet. facetime a loved one.
	Free Time	Set a time limit and use a gadget for positive task.
	Bed Time	Brush your teeth.

4.5 Self-Management and Its Relationship to Emotional Intelligence

Emotional intelligence is known as the capacity to recognize, use, and regulate your own emotions to reduce stress, communicate, sympathize with others, overcome obstacles, and diffuse conflict. You can develop stronger relationships, perform well at work and school, and reach your professional and personal goals with the aid of emotional intelligence. Additionally, it can assist you in establishing a connection with your emotions, putting your intentions into practice, and choosing what is most important to you.

Chapter 5: Executive Skills Activities for Teens

Our brains' executive functioning mechanisms enable us to carry out daily duties. They include our capacity for task prioritization, material organization, activity focus, and grit under pressure. These abilities are crucial, which should go without saying. We utilize these abilities frequently each day without even realizing it. By just reading this article, you are engaging your focus, metacognitive strategies, and working memory.

5.1 Executive Assessment

Executive Assessments are very important, especially for active teens. It evaluates your preparation for school. Appreciates the expertise and practical experience you will bring and enables you to use your findings to improve your abilities.

5.2 Schedule Your Time

A solid routine can give your kid a sense of stability and security while facilitating better time management so they can balance the demands of school, friends, employment, play, and study.

5.3 Understanding Your Feelings

Our interpersonal relationships improve as a result. That is because being aware of our emotions can make communicating how we feel, avoiding conflict, and dealing with difficult emotions simpler.

Explore Yourself

Q. Complete the sentence.

a. I feel happy when _____

_____

b. I feel sad when _____

_____

c. I feel angry when _____

_____

d. I feel excited when _____

_____

e. I feel surprised when _____

_____

5.4 Explore Yourself

Exploring yourself is very important to control yourself. It helps you manage your emotions and expressions when you closely monitor them and know them deeply.

Explore Yourself

My favorite color is	My favorite subject is	I am most happy when I
My favorite activity is	My favorite food is	I really hate it when
I really want to be	Most people don't know that I	If I had a million dollar
My goal of life is	Right now, I feel very	My favorite memory is

2 truths & a lie about my life

1. _____
2. _____
3. _____

5.5 Complement Me

People want to be around you and feel good when you give them compliments. Giving praise is a powerful way to influence others since those around them are likelier to follow your lead and pay attention to your ideas.

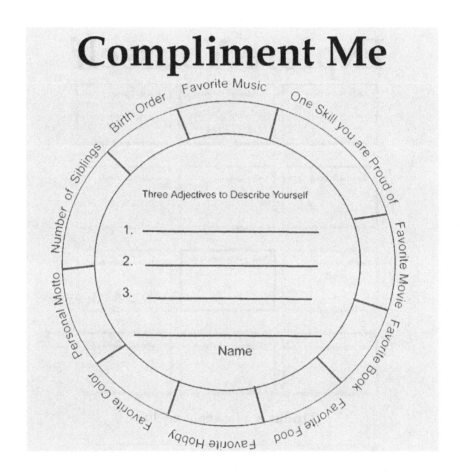

5.6 My Coping Steps

Coping mechanisms assist you in enduring, minimizing, and managing stressful circumstances. Effective stress management can improve your physical and mental health and your capacity for peak performance.

My Coping Steps

Some things that make me stressed are:

1.
2.
3.

These changes happen when I feel stressed:

Changes in my body	Thoughts I have	Things I do

When i feel stressed, my strategy is:

_____

_____

What other strategies I can use to best cope
my stress:

_____

_____

5.7 My Positive Talk Journal

By assisting you in prioritizing issues, worries, and concerns, journaling helps you to control your emotions and elevate your mood. Keeping a daily log of any symptoms will help you identify triggers and figure out how to manage them effectively.

Positive Talk Journal

Common Negative thoughts I usually have are:

Questions to ask myself:

Is this thought true?   **Do I have supporting evidence that it is true?**

What is the worst that can happen?

What best can happen?

What is the reason of this thought?

Am I responsible for this thought?

Should I keep thinking like that?

5.8 Gratitude Journal

Teenagers can maintain composure and center themselves in turbulent times by keeping a gratitude notebook. It's a simple habit to form that will benefit you in the long run.

Use it to write a daily gratitude journal to keep you grateful.

Daily Gratitude

Activities

Priorities:

Notes

Affirmations

5.9 Executive Functioning Wheel

Children learn teamwork, leadership, decision-making, goal-setting, critical thinking, adaptation, and emotional awareness through the development of their executive abilities.

Conclusion

People and society gain for the rest of their lives when youngsters are given a chance to develop executive function and self-regulation skills successfully.

Executive function abilities aid students in following complicated instructions, avoiding distractions, readjusting when rules change, persevering with problem-solving, and managing lengthy tasks. The result is a population that is more educated and prepared to handle the problems of the twenty-first century for society.

Executive functions assist young people in acquiring abilities such as collaboration, leadership, goal-setting, decision-making, critical thinking, flexibility, and self-awareness of one's own and others' emotions. Greater social cohesion, less crime, and more stable communities are the results for society.

Executive function abilities assist people in making wiser decisions regarding their diet and exercise, being more mindful of safety for ourselves and our children, and rejecting encouragement to take risks, try drugs, or have unprotected activities. Having strong executive function prepares our bodies and coping mechanisms to handle stress. A healthier population, a more effective workforce, and lower healthcare expenses are the results for society.

Executive function abilities increase our capacity for economic success because they enable us to be more organized, handle problems that call for planning, and be ready to adapt to changing conditions. Greater wealth for society is the result of a workforce that is creative, skilled, and adaptable.

Made in United States
North Haven, CT
09 October 2023

42561076R00029